Two of my buddies from St. James: ten-year-old Keith Lavia and his two-year-old brother Dugal, photographed near their home in the village of Sea View

To
the people of Barbados,
with affection and admiration
for the world they have created

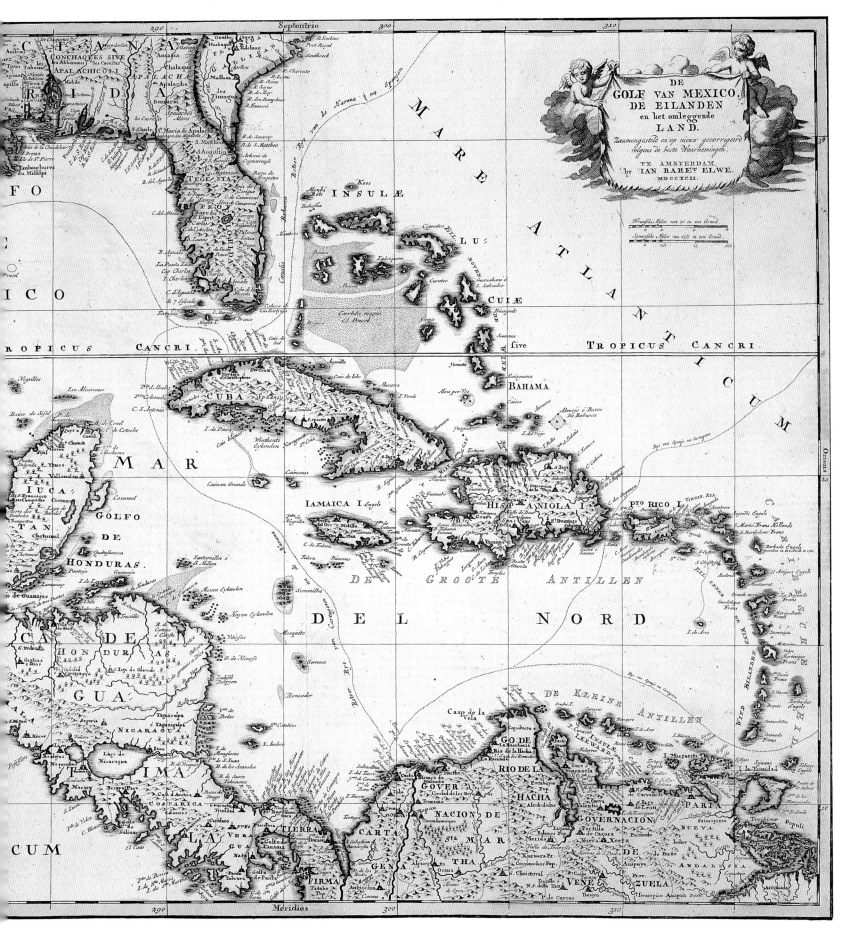

An 18th-century Dutch map of the Caribbean; Barbados, extreme right, is "Barbadas, Engels [English]"

A sunset sky silhouettes coconut palms on the west coast.

Barbados
A World Apart

Text and photographs by

Roger A. LaBrucherie

Imágenes Press

Born of necessity, the transportable chattel house dates from the 19th century, when plantation laborers were unable to buy land and might be forced to move from their rented "house spots" on short notice. Of that necessity has grown Barbados' most endearing architectural style, a style in danger of disappearing as Bajans move on to larger and more permanent homes.

Contents

"This singular island . . ."

Since this is now my third book on Barbados, it would be foolish of me to deny that I have developed a love affair with this island. Although I sometimes find it dismaying to think of it, a decade and a half have passed since my first visit to Barbados. From that original encounter came my first collection of impressions about the island and her people, entitled *Images of Barbados*. In 1982, four years and several visits later, there followed a more ambitious book, entitled *A Barbados Journey*, in which I attempted a more thorough and systematic presentation of the island.

As is true with most things in life, books begin to show their age after a time; and for the past three or four years I have been wanting to do an update of *Barbados Journey*, and made several extended visits to the island to take new photographs for such a revision. Each time I was about ready to start the revising process, however, another project intervened, and the Barbados project was delayed. Thus by the time I was finally ready to go forward with the update, I had gathered so much new material that an entirely new book seemed appropriate.

Those familiar with my two earlier works on Barbados will see that this book combines the approaches of the first two: for while the selection of photographs is personal and impressionistic, I have also attempted to give the book a logical framework which will convey a great deal of information about the island and its history. Hopefully the result fulfills the ambition that I have always held for my books: that they be more than just collections of pretty pictures, and that they educate as well as entertain. It is for this reason that I call them documentary books, and I have always hoped that they might serve as bridges to understanding in a world in which people of differing cultures and backgrounds increasingly come into contact with one another.

One result of my extended and repeated encounters with Barbados over the past fifteen years has been my own growing realization that, the better I have come to know the island, the more complex I have realized her culture and society to be. While I harbor no illusions that I will ever fully understand this singular island and her people, neither, after such a lengthy acquaintance, can I conceive of the day when Barbados will no longer be a part of my life. God willing, I will have the pleasure of getting to know the island and her people better for many years to come.

Superb Cave Bay on the south coast in St. Philip Parish

Viewed from Cherry Tree Hill, the Scotland District of St. Andrew is perhaps the most dramatic and photographed landscape on the island [this page]. An aerial view of the west coast near Holetown reveals why the St. James shoreline is referred to as the "Gold Coast" [opposite page].

Much of Barbados' agricultural work is done by women, such as Miss Velda Small, whom I photographed early one morning on her way to a day of hoeing sweet potatoes near her home in the St. George Valley [this page].

Ready to start the day in her bright blue school dress, eight-year old Shaunna Yearwood plays outside her home in Lowlands, St. Lucy [opposite page]. Barbados provides free, universal, and compulsory education to the age of sixteen; if youngsters qualify, they may be entitled to free post-secondary education as well. The result of the country's emphasis on education is one of the highest literacy rates in the world, and the best-educated population in the Caribbean.

As the seventeenth-century planters grew wealthy on the profits from sugar, they built plantation "great houses" suited to their new station in life. Among the oldest of these houses, and certainly the most striking, is St. Nicholas Abbey in St. Peter, dating from about 1650 [this page].

The stone construction and architectural style of Heron Bay, a superb holiday house on the west coast [opposite page], also suggest great antiquity. Despite appearances, the house was built in 1947 by Ronald Tree, who was the driving force behind the establishment of the Barbados National Trust.

Decked out in ceremonial dress, members of the Mounted Troop of the Royal Barbados Police Force [this page], prepare for an appearance at the annual Opening of Parliament.

Although his uniform is modern, Sergeant Neville Brathwaite of the Barbados Defense Force [opposite page] stands in a long line of military tradition, for the island has a history of military units dating back to the earliest decades of the colony. The role of the Defense Force is the defense of the island from external attack, but a long list of Barbadians distinguished themselves in service abroad during both World Wars.

The magnificent east coast in early morning light, from Cattlewash, St. Joseph

A west coast stroller finds a bit of solitude on Turtle Beach, St. Peter.

Retired broommaker Arrington Johnson, 68, gazes into the camera in the doorway of his home in Road View, St. Peter [opposite page]. The country's excellent school system promises a wider future for these high school students I encountered in Belleplaine [this page]. As is the case with many Barbadians, the youngsters were at first reluctant to be photographed, but when I explained my purpose, they happily had a collective change of mind, and this picture resulted.

Standing serenely at the end of a row of cabbage palms, Codrington College commands a superb view overlooking Conset Bay in St. John [this page]. A theological institution for the training of West Indian clergy, the college was built in the first half of the eighteenth century from the bequest of Christopher Codrington, a wealthy St. John plantation owner.

Dubbed the "Gold Coast" for its deluxe resorts and grand vacation homes, the island's west coast has many lesser known architectural gems as well, such as this elegant guest cottage at Maddox House in St. James [opposite page].

Some of the island's most "ordinary" flowers are also its most beautiful: a hibiscus decorates a garden in St. Thomas [opposite page]. Another pretty island resident, the yellow-breast, frequently joins outdoor diners without waiting for a formal invitation [this page].

A series of exquisite small beaches fringe the flat expanses of St. Philip Parish in the southeastern corner of the island.

Beginnings

Floating at the edge of their crystalline blue sea, they lie in a sweeping gem-like arc stretching from South America to Florida, these islands called the West Indies. Seemingly too small and fragile to have long withstood the pounding waves of the vast Atlantic, their presence has nonetheless sheltered and defined the waters of the Caribbean Sea for tens of millions of years. The tops of mighty undersea mountains, the islands owe their existence to plate tectonics, the glacially-slow movement of the enormous segments of rock which form the earth's crust. Along the line of the bulging curve where the Caribbean Plate joins the American Plate, a combination of volcanic, folding, and scraping forces have lifted the sea floor to form the chain of the Lesser Antilles.

Barbados itself, however, is little more than a half million years old, vastly younger than the other Windward Islands, which are volcanic in origin. Barbados' base is not volcanic, but rather was uplifted by the scraping and folding of the sea floor as one plate overrode the other. Then, as the level of the sea rose and fell over the eons in response to the changing size of the polar ice caps, and periodic upliftings of the island continued, a coral reef some 250 feet thick was added to the top of this undersea mountain—formed from the skeletal remains of countless coral polyps.

Later still, after the top of this mountain was lifted above the level of the sea, the central part of the island was tilted, so that the surface rises gently away from the West Coast to about the middle of the island, where it reaches Barbados' highest elevation at Mt. Hillaby (1116'). There the coral cap breaks, and the island falls dramatically toward the Atlantic shore in the precipitous slopes of the Scotland District, where tropical rains borne by the trade winds have ceaselessly eroded the underlying sedimentary rock.

Where the coral cap remained, however, as it did over most of the island, the porous limestone rock absorbed those rains, carving the surface into a landscape of rolling hills traversed here and there by deep gullies, and concealing huge caverns carved by subterranean streams and rivers carrying the rainfall to the sea. Wind and current, and later, birds of passage, brought seeds, and in time a dense forest—including the cabbage palm, destined

The sea has pounded ceaselessly on Barbados' coastline for countless millennia, carving cliffs and beaches from the island's coral and underlying sedimentary rock. But timeless-looking scenes like this one at Bathsheba, where rocks frame the rising sun [opposite page] are deceptive, for these "sea stacks" are in fact remnants of an ancient shoreline.

A few miles up the coast, at Pie Corner in St. Lucy, stands further graphic evidence of the island's many shorelines over the course of its history: one hundred feet above sea level, in the midst of a cow pasture, stands another sea stack— its undercut base bearing testimony to the waves which eons ago crashed against the rock [this page].

to become one of the symbols of Barbados—covered the moister parts of the island.

As this lush paradise took form, birds and insects, carried perhaps by fierce winds from neighboring islands or the South American continent, reached the island and made it their home. At great intervals, lizards, iguanas, one species of tree frog, and a handful of mammals—notably the raccoon—overcame incredible odds, survived a driftwood-aided sea journey and established themselves on the island. And so, over the vastness of unrecorded time, this island world took shape, pristine in its protecting sea.

Worlds away, perhaps 400,000 years ago, the earliest beings we call humans were evolving and spreading across Africa, Asia, and Europe. Only much later, perhaps twelve thousand years before

Christ, did the first Asian tribes venture across the land bridge which from time to time linked Siberia with Alaska, and begin spreading throughout the Americas.

Just when the first of these continental peoples began exploring the islands of the Caribbean it is impossible to say with precision, but extensive archaeological evidence suggests that a people of the Arawak culture who made their home in the Saladero-Barrancas region of the Orinoco River valley of Venezuela had settled the Lesser Antilles, including Barbados, around the time of Christ.

The Arawaks were at home on the sea, travelling and trading up and down the island chain in large dugout canoes, some of which were capable of carrying forty men or more. This facility with sea travel meant that no island was culturally

The island's highly porous coral surface absorbs most of the rainfall like a sponge, so Barbados has no permanent surface rivers. But deep underground this rainwater has carved channels through the limestone as it makes its way to the sea, and in places these subterranean rivers have created large caverns. The most dramatic is Harrison's Cave, in St. Thomas, known to island residents in past centuries, then forgotten. Only rediscovered in the early 1970s, the cave has recently been developed into the island's most popular tourist attraction.

Erosion of the coral by wave action has created a varied shoreline, including this secluded cove beach at Cave Bay in St. Philip [opposite page].

As is the case with nearly all islands, Barbados had relatively few species of flora and fauna before the arrival of mankind. Even the coconut palm [this page], so universally identified with the tropics, is thought to have originated in southeast Asia, and may have been introduced to the Caribbean by Europeans. The tiny whistling tree frog, on the other hand, famous throughout the Caribbean for its nighttime cricket-like call, is indigenous to the island. [Actual size of Eleutherodactylus johnstonei: about 3/4" in length]

Amerindian peoples from South America, traveling in large ocean-going dugout canoes, began settling the Caribbean around the time of Christ, and possibly considerably before. Because the native populations of the islands were almost completely wiped out soon after European contact, the archaeological record (including some superb pottery artifacts, opposite page), supplies most of what is known of the pre-Columbian peoples who inhabited the area. By the time the English arrived to colonize Barbados in 1627, there were no Indians left on the island.

isolated from its neighbors, and the culture the Arawaks developed was to a great extent common throughout the entire Caribbean basin. Thus, much of what is known about the Amerindian culture on Barbados is derived from artifacts found not only on Barbados itself, but from the artifacts and anthropological evidence of other islands throughout the Caribbean. (One aspect of the Amerindian culture on Barbados does appear to be unique to the island, however: since the island lacked a native stone of sufficient hardness for tool-making, the Arawaks fashioned a wide variety of tools from the conch shells which they found in abundance in the surrounding waters.)

From this body of evidence, the Arawaks of Barbados are believed to have developed an extensive agriculture based on native New World plants such as peanuts, papaya, squash, peppers, and perhaps maize and cotton. Undoubtedly the most important part of the Arawak diet, however, was cassava (manioc), which was processed to remove its poisonous juice, then ground and cooked as a griddlecake. Since fish was also a vital part of their diet and because they lacked draft animals and plows, most of the Arawak villages were located in easily cultivated sites near the coast and sources of fresh water.

Pottery artifacts discovered at various sites on Barbados—including Chancery Lane and Silver Sands (both near the southern shore in the Parish of Christ Church) as well as at Pie Corner (near the east coast in St. Lucy)—suggest that Amerindian peoples occupied Barbados more or less continuously for the next fifteen centuries—that is, through the time of the discovery of the West Indies by Columbus.

Archaeological excavations in Barbados have uncovered the remains of dozens of coastal Indian villages, many of them near the northern tip of the island, where sixty-foot cliffs offered a natural defence against enemy attack [this page]. The sea also supplied a good part of the Amerindians' diet, although they were accomplished farmers as well. In Barbados, as on the other islands of the Caribbean, they likely grew such New World crops as squash, peanuts, peppers, papaya, maize, and, above all, cassava. Ground and cooked as a griddlecake, cassava (also known as manioc), was the staple food of the Amerindians throughout the Caribbean.

What remains unclear from the archeological record is whether a competing Amerindian group called the Caribs (who have, of course, given their name to the region) were the last occupants of Barbados before the English settlement, or whether the Arawaks themselves occupied the island right up to the time of European contact. Conventional archeological wisdom attributes a fierce, warlike nature to the Caribs, and they are thought to have battled with the Arawaks for dominance in the Caribbean for some three centuries preceding Columbus's arrival.

One oft-cited basis for a Carib presence on Barbados is sociological: there is evidence that during the sixteenth century the Spanish enslaved Amerindian inhabitants of Barbados (as they enslaved the inhabitants of many of the Lesser Antilles) to work their mines and farms on Hispaniola, Puerto Rico, and Cuba. It is also known that official Spanish policy, at least after 1511, exempted the Arawaks from such enslavement; hence, the argument goes, the Indians on Barbados in the early 1500s must have been Caribs. This is, however, a very slender reed to support the theory of a Carib presence on Barbados. However well-intentioned the official Spanish policy, the fact is that in practice virtually all the Indians of the Caribbean, Arawaks and Caribs alike, were at the mercy of the *conquistadores* in search of free labor.

Given the necessarily tenuous nature of archaeology, the history of the Amerindians on Barbados will perhaps never be clear. What *is* clear is that throughout the Caribbean and the Americas the conquering European powers had little respect for the peoples and cultures they encountered, and even less for those peoples' claim to the lands they inhabited. The Amerindian peoples were routinely enslaved, overworked, and sometimes murdered outright. Even more devastating was the effect of European diseases such as measles and smallpox on Indian populations who had developed no immunity to them. In most cases these combined calamities wiped out the entire indigenous populations of the Caribbean islands within a few decades of European contact.

What is also clear is that when the Portuguese navigator Pedro A. Campos visited the island in 1536, he found the island uninhabited. (The Spanish and Portuguese had dubbed the island *Los Barbados,* perhaps, it is theorized, after the aerial roots of the "bearded" fig trees native to the island.) Some researchers believe that when the Amerindian population, whether it was Arawak or Carib, began to understand the threat posed by the Europeans, they fled to the greater safety offered by the expanses of the South American continent, their ancestral homeland. Despite their presence on Barbados for fifteen centuries, the Amerindians left little lasting trace on the island, and so it is easy to forget that they called Barbados home for a much longer time than has the present Euro-African civilization. (Ironically, the best known reminder of the pre-European civilization on the island is one which is almost never associated with the Amerindians. But in fact the name of Barbados' capital, Bridgetown, derives from the crude Indian bridge the English discovered at the site when they arrived to found their colony in 1627; indeed, in the early years one alternative name for the settlement was "The Indian Bridge Town.")

Although both the Portuguese and the Spanish made sporadic visits to Barbados during the 1500s, neither made any effort to settle it, probably because they had their hands full with their other New World colonies. And so the island, after having known human civilization for perhaps fifteen centuries, now would lie quietly for another century, without human habitation.

England & Africa

Although their island home had long made the English familiar with the sea, it was the Portuguese and, by a stroke of luck, the Spanish, who ventured first and farthest beyond Europe's waters. It was that Spanish luck, in the form of underwriting Columbus's obsession with finding the westward route to the fabled Indies, that had made the Caribbean a Spanish lake for more than a century after the Great Admiral's monumental voyage of 1492.

Determined not to be outdistanced by her longtime rival, England also sent explorers westward in search of a route to Asia and riches to fill the royal coffers. Like Columbus, England's explorers were stymied by lands hitherto unknown to Europe—in their case, the North American continent. Eventually, in the 1600s, English settlers would set out to colonize lands which would become known as Virginia, Massachusetts, Pennsylvania . . ..

By the time England turned her attention south, the richest island prizes—Cuba, Hispaniola, Puerto Rico, Jamaica—not to mention all the continental land touching on the Caribbean, were firmly in Spanish hands. But with an entire continent to deal with, Spain had not had the resources to colonize every island in the Caribbean. Thus in 1624 English settlers were able to found a colony on the island of St. Christopher (St. Kitts). A year later, on May 14th, 1625, en route home from a voyage to Brazil, Captain John Powell chanced upon Barbados, landed on the west coast, and finding the island uninhabited, claimed Barbados for King James I of England.

Two years later, on February 17, 1627, some eighty colonists under the sponsorship of a London merchant and world trader, Sir William Courteen (Captain Powell's employer), returned to the West Coast and named their new settlement Jamestown. The town would eventually take on the name of the geographical feature which made it attractive to settlement, a "hole" where a small fresh water stream flowed into the sea—thus was "Holetown" born.

Courteen's colonial venture was intended to

Claimed for England in 1625, settled in 1627, within a decade of its founding the colony had discovered the crop which would mold its future: sugar cane. (The photograph on the opposite page shows the semi-refined, or "dark crystal," sugar produced in Barbados.) With a fertile soil and tropical sun and rain, the island lacked only one essential element: a large supply of cheap labor. The solution to that problem was found in Africa and the institution of slavery, which too would dominate the island's future. Between 1627 and 1807, when England abolished the slave trade, tens of thousands of African slaves were brought to the island in abominable conditions in the holds of slave ships [this page].

turn a profit for himself and his partners by producing agricultural crops for export, but the immediate task facing the settlers was to ensure the viability of the colony by growing enough food for their own survival. With the help of about 40 Arawak Indians brought from Dutch Guyana—and ten African slaves taken from a slave trading ship on the colonizing voyage out from England—they set to work clearing land and planting traditional Arawak crops such as cassava, yams, maize, and plantain. Their efforts bore fruit: the flow of additional settlers to the colony was large and rapid, and the success of Courteen's gamble seemed assured. Instead, within two years Courteen and his partners had been completely dispossessed of their fledgling colony, in the "Great Barbados Robbery," and the island was in a state of turmoil as two competing factions vied for supremacy.

To say that the details of Courteen's loss are convoluted is to risk being guilty of understatement in the extreme. Stated very simply, despite Courteen's colonizing settlement, the Earl of Carlisle, a favorite of James I, succeeded in obtaining from the King a grant of proprietorship to the "Caribbee Islands," which included Barbados. Acting on this grant, in the summer of 1628 a group of settlers led by Charles Wolverston (who had been appointed Governor of the island by the Carlisle faction) arrived and established a settlement at the Indian Bridge (today's Bridgetown), some eight miles south of the Courteen settlement. With two groups of settlers and two Governors under competing claims of right, tension and conflict were inevitable, and nearly led to armed hostilities. Although the dispute was formally ended in favor of Carlisle's grant in May of 1629, the ill feeling between the two groups would taint the colony for years to come. [The full details of the Courteen-Carlisle dispute are beyond the scope of a general historical overview such as this; for the reader wanting a more extensive treatment, F. A. Hoyos' *Barbados* is an excellent source.]

Despite these political machinations, as the colony neared the end of its first decade the population of the island had grown to perhaps 12,000 people, and the settlers were growing tobacco, cotton, and ginger for export. The island's arable land was for the most part divided into hundreds of small farms, producing a mixture of export crops as well as fruits and vegetables for local consumption. And while the colony counted perhaps as many as eight hundred African slaves, the great majority of the population was made up of English settlers, many of them indentured servants who had accepted their indenture as the price of passage and a new start in the New World, or criminals who had chosen indenture in the colonies rather than more severe punishment in England.

Enter sugar, and slavery

Then, in 1637, a new crop was brought to the island from Brazil: sugar cane. A member of the grass family, sugar cane had been introduced to Brazil by the Portuguese in the middle of the 16th century, and Brazilian growers had grown wealthy satisfying the developing European taste for sweets. Sugar cane would prove ideally suited to the climatic and soil conditions of Barbados and would, in the span of two or three decades, radically alter the face and development of Barbados for all time. (The best long-term indication of sugar cane's suitability to the island is the fact that despite repeated efforts over the three and a half centuries since cane's introduction, Barbadians have not, to this day, found a crop better adapted to their island.)

Sugar cane was so well suited to Barbados' conditions—and so profitable to its growers—that the value of arable land multiplied astronomically in the decade following its introduction. One example cited in *A true and exact History of the Island of Barbados*, the very first history of the island, published by Richard Ligon in 1657, suggests that the potential profits from sugar production multiplied the price of plantation land more than thirty-fold. The owners of arable land who saw the value of their holdings skyrocket virtually overnight were doubtless well-pleased at their good fortune. But for most property owners, as well as for the population at large, the introduction of sugar cane was to have longer-term implications for the colony which were almost certainly not foreseen.

Although the profits from sugar production were potentially great, successful cultivation required a great deal of capital. Sugar cane is slow to mature, requiring 14–16 months from planting to harvest, during which time the crop produces no income. Furthermore, the extraction of the juice from the cane and its processing to produce crystalline sugar required both knowledge (what we would today call technology) and expensive machinery. Both of these factors favored the wealthy; the second doubly favored the larger landowners (most of whom were among the wealthy), since the costs would be minimized when spread over more acreage and greater production. The combined result of these factors was the beginning of the consolidation of landholding into the hands of fewer owners, as the economics of sugar production took their toll on Barbados' yeoman farmers.

Aside from the requirement of capital, sugar cane cultivation required a great deal of manual labor, much of it very hard work. It was doubtless not very appealing as wage-paying labor to those small farmers who were being displaced from their land, nor to the English indentured servants, who were in any case in short supply. Thus the planters faced a serious problem at the outset: a large and reliable supply of cheap labor.

There was a ready answer to this dilemma, however, in the form of African slave labor. Virtually from the first days of their colonization of the New World the Spanish and Portuguese had enslaved the native Indians, whom they regarded as something less than human, to perform the tasks the colonizers were unable or unwilling to do. Within a few decades that source of free labor had virtually disappeared, however, as the Amerindian population fell victim to overwork, European diseases, and in some cases outright slaughter. But the habit and pattern had been established, and as the natives died out, the colonizers turned to Africa as their new source of cheap labor.

As long as Barbados was a colony made up of small holders working their own land, slaves had had a limited appeal, and formed a small minority of the population. But the introduction of sugar cane and the hard physical labor it demanded, together with the concentration of arable land into ever fewer plantations, changed everything. Now African slaves became the ideal solution to the planters' labor needs: for although the purchase of a slave required a large initial expenditure (again favoring the planter with capital), once acquired, slaves could be forced to work far harder—and at less cost—than a worker free to seek another job, or worse yet, to leave the island altogether.

Thus in the decades following the introduction of sugar cane, arable land became increasingly concentrated into fewer and larger plantations, where the work was increasingly done by African slaves. A few stark figures tell the story: in 1640, before the sugar culture had taken hold, the island popu-

lation stood at little more than 30,000 people, of which fewer than a thousand were African slaves. Four decades later, in the 1680s, there were forty to fifty thousand black slaves on the island, while the white population had shrunk to about 20,000 inhabitants. As the sugar culture evolved and came to monopolize the arable land, the free white settlers, unable to earn a decent living in a slave-dominated economy, sought a better life abroad. By the end of the 17th century perhaps as many as 30,000 whites had emigrated to other colonies in the Caribbean or North America. (Many of these emigrants settled in South Carolina, where Barbadians would be instrumental in establishing the new English colony.)

As the sugar monoculture developed, the concentration of economic power in the hands of a few landowners inevitably had consequences in the political realm as well. Since 1639, the colony had enjoyed a measure of representative government when the House of Burgesses (later called the House of Assembly) had been established as an essentially advisory body to the Governor. Then, in 1652, during the time of the English Civil War, the Assembly's control over taxation had been acknowledged in the "Charter of Barbados," which settled an armed clash between the island's mainly pro-royalist leadership and Oliver Cromwell's Commonwealth. And while the House of Assembly had never been elected by the whole of Barbadian society (there being a property qualification which limited the vote to a tiny minority of the population), in the earlier days of the colony the Assembly represented a fairly homogeneous population.

So well suited was sugar cane to Barbados that within a few decades of its introduction sugar cultivation dominated the economy and the landscape as well, creating a carpet of green. (The photograph above is of cane fields in St. George Parish in the early 1990s.) The consolidation of economic power into a few hands created a "plantocracy" under which the big planters effectively ruled the island through their control of the island's legislature and the governor appointed by London. (The painting on the opposite page entitled "Governor Robinson Going to Church" depicts farmland surrounding Bridgetown and a flotilla crowding Carlisle Bay in the early eighteen century.)

But as the plantation system evolved during the 1700s there emerged a highly stratified society with the wealthy planter families at the top, and at the bottom a large and growing mass of African slaves outnumbering the white population by three or four to one. Although a sizeable lower middle class of white tradesmen, professionals, small farmers, and merchants remained on the island, the property requirement for voting effectively limited the island's political power to the "plantocracy," as the plantation owners came to be called.

Thus, as Barbados moved into the 18th century, it settled into a classic plantation- and slavery-based society, dominated, politically, economically, and socially by a tiny minority composed of white planters. This sugar society reached its high point about 1700; the remainder of the century was to see a slow decline (masked, to be sure, by cyclical short-term swings) of Barbados' sugar fortunes, as soil depletion, trade disruptions, competition from other sugar-producing colonies, and—in the last part of the century—competition from a new discovery, beet sugar, took their toll.

The backbone of this sugar economy, and the colony's Achilles' heel, was of course the island's slave population. The danger presented by the slave system had been brought home forcefully in 1675, when a plotted slave uprising was discovered before it could be put into effect, and nearly a score of the leaders were executed. Further plots or "scares" of slave rebellions occurred in the 1680s and '90s, and again in 1702, all of which were met with severe punishment, in an attempt to deter further outbreaks. This may explain why the colony passed virtually the entire 18th century without further attempts at slave rebellion. But the absence of outright rebellion during the 1700s disguises the fact that slavery in Barbados was in a state of flux throughout the 1700s, and that there

were forces at work which would, in the first third of the 19th century, bring the demise of slavery in Barbados and throughout the English colonies.

Those forces were at work within not only the white society (in Barbados and in the outside world) but within the slave population as well. The institution of slavery had of course been known to the European world long before the colonization of Barbados, and it is not surprising that the plantocracy accepted slavery as a natural and necessary phenomenon, since it was so well suited to their economic interests. Furthermore, to the extent that slavery depended on the perception that the slave was subhuman, the condition of slaves recently arrived from Africa made that perception all the easier to hold: they were black, and therefore different from their masters. They also came from a culture vastly different from Europe's, which accentuated their "difference." Perhaps most vital of all, they spoke no English, and thus could not understand much of the world around them; nor could the white population—had they wanted to—enter the minds of the slaves. Thus the Africans were reduced to their most elemental selves—their physical bodies—which was the only element the plantation economy valued.

But, as the years passed, Barbados' slave population changed: of necessity, the slaves learned and adapted to the ways of European culture. New generations of slaves, born in Barbados, had no direct knowledge of Africa, grew up speaking more English than their parents, and acculturated to a higher degree. In short, the slaves were becoming "creolized," and in so doing, becoming less "different" from their masters.

Over years of contact, the white man's perception of the slaves began to change as well: initially seen as little more than beasts in human shells, as the slaves acquired the ability to communicate and

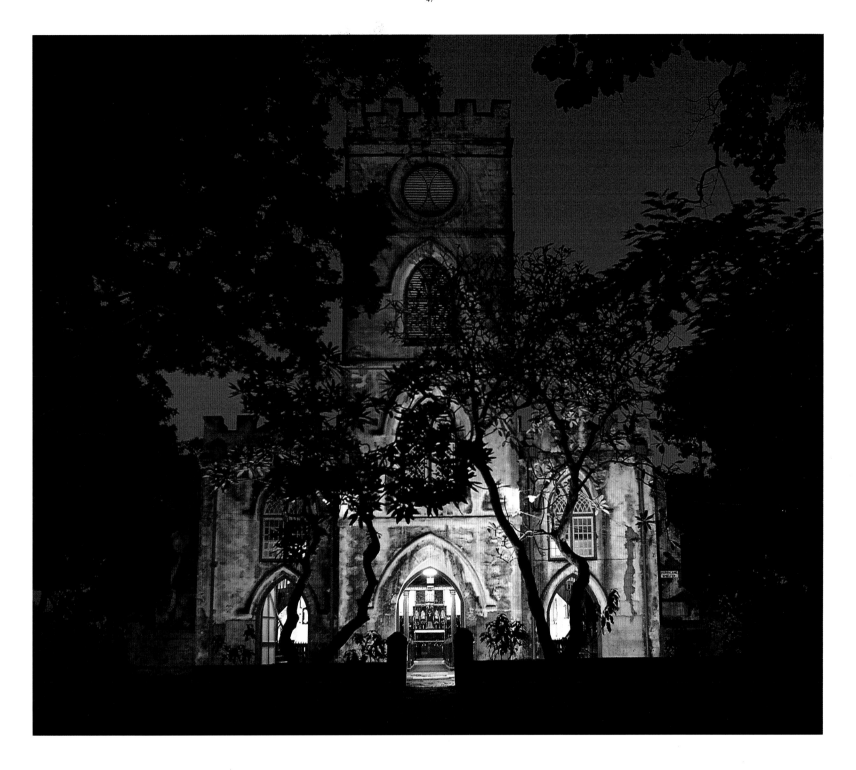

The spread of sugar cane over the countryside created a landscape reminding the colonists of England's West Country, and they took to calling the island "Little England." The stone churches built in each of the eleven parishes would complete the tableau. St. John's Church, rebuilt (for the fourth time) after the great hurricane of 1831, still commands a glorious view from its vantage point high above the East Coast.

As the value of her colonies in the Caribbean grew during the 17th and 18th centuries, England fortified the islands against her enemies (principally the French and Spanish) and built a series of forts to guard the vulnerable south and west coasts. The headquarters for the four thousand British troops was at St. Ann's Fort, east of Bridgetown. The Main Guard, with its imposing clock tower [this page], dates from about 1803 and still overlooks the Garrison Savannah, where the imperial troops paraded in the colonial era [opposite page].

For the slaves of the colony, home was not a plantation great house, but a slave hut, originally built of wattle and daub, then later of the island's native stone. (A scant handful of the stone huts, similar to the house shown here, survive to this day.) The slaves' lot was without question a hard one, but it was not without relief, especially in the later years of the slave era: Sunday was the day of rest, and Sunday dances on the plantations became a tradition.

interact mentally with their masters, they began to be recognized as human beings—albeit perhaps unconsciously and unwillingly. In short, the mental preconception which underpins the institution of slavery was being gradually eroded.

Other factors also influenced these perceptions. As the years passed, a number of slaves gained their legal freedom, creating a new category in Barbadian society: the free coloureds. For the slave population, the existence of these free Africans in Barbados was a constant reminder that slavery was not a natural consequence of their blackness, but rather a social condition which had been imposed upon them. As for the slave masters, it was impossible for them to ignore the growing sentiment led by the abolitionist movement overseas, especially in their revered Mother Country, that slavery was

an immoral institution. (The formal expression of this growing sentiment was the outlawing of slavery within England—although not her colonies—in 1772.)

Not surprisingly, the anti-slavery movement was led by organized religion, especially the Quaker, Wesleyan, and Moravian churches. The Anglican Church was slower to endorse a change which would so drastically affect the fortunes of the planter class, but, by the turn of the century, it had become a powerful force in the abolitionist movement. As the century drew to a close, then, the stage was being set for an end to the institution which had become part and parcel of Barbados' existence.

The abolitionist movement was far from the only "foreign" development whose influence

Although sugar cane brought a relative prosperity to Barbados, it was a prosperity borne on the backs of the slaves who comprised the overwhelming majority of the island's population.

The slaves attempted revolt a number of times in the 1600s, and once again in 1702; all these plots were discovered and crushed before they could be put into action, with horrible punishments for the rebels. Then over a century passed without an attempted uprising; but any thoughts that the slaves were contented with their lot evaporated in 1816 when the slaves rose up in what has come to be called "Bussa's Rebellion." During the course of the fighting and in the executions that followed, several hundred slaves lost their lives in this last attempt to throw off their shackles. Two decades later the slaves gained their freedom when the British Parliament abolished slavery throughout British territory.

Although Barbadians may not have realized it at the time, with emancipation Barbados had begun a long journey which would lead from colony to nation. At a roundabout on the ABC Highway, a heroic bronze "Slave in Revolt" (seen here photographed with a double exposure) sculpted by the artist Karl Broodhagen, commemorates the slaves' long struggle for freedom and their long-awaited Emancipation Day, August 1, 1834.

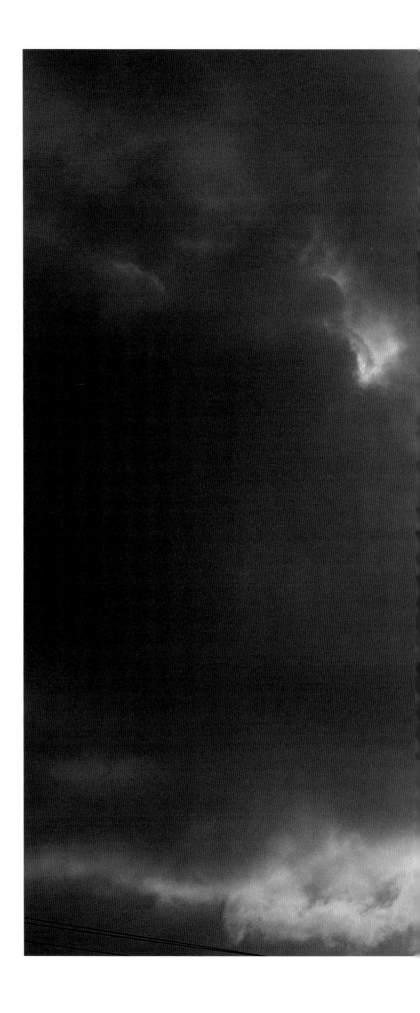

would be felt in Barbados. The 1700s have been referred to as the "Century of Wars," and during its course (and indeed well into the 19th century) England found herself repeatedly embroiled in conflicts which would also affect "Little England" (as Barbadians had taken to calling their island). The best known to Americans was the War of Independence between England and her Thirteen Colonies: although not directly involving Barbados, the outbreak of hostilities in 1775 brought considerable hardship to the colony because it meant the closing of the North American trade on which Barbados had come to rely heavily for supplying the everyday necessities of life. English wars with France, Holland, and Spain followed soon after, and here, in addition to the disruption to trade, the Caribbean figured directly as an area of conflict, as the opposing forces sought to capture the island colonies of their enemies.

Protected by numerous forts and batteries along its south and west coasts, as well as by its encircling coral reef, Barbados was virtually alone in the Caribbean in being free from attack during this period. (Indeed, Barbados enjoys the distinction of having never been invaded by a foreign army throughout its history. Undoubtedly, as has often been pointed out, the island's location upwind of the other Leeward Islands made invasion difficult in the era of square-rigged warships. But perhaps luck and the island's strong garrison (some 4000 regular troops plus another 5000 men in the militia) played a role as well: nearby St. Lucia, hotly contested by the British and French, changed hands more than a dozen times.)

As Barbados entered the 1800s, change and reform were unmistakably in the air. The latter half of the 18th century had seen a further decline in the fortunes of the sugar industry, and in 1807 the British Parliament dealt it a further blow by abolishing the slave trade throughout the British colonies, a move which was seen as a prelude to the abolition of slavery itself. Then, in 1816, there occurred the largest slave rebellion in Barbados' history, during which some 175 slaves and one white were killed and a great deal of property, including about a fifth of the sugar crop, was destroyed. Although the rioting was put down (with the execution of over 200 slave rioters), the tragedy added fuel to the emancipationists' zeal and made it clear to all that Barbadian life rested on a powder keg.

Nonetheless, the slave owners, wedded as ever to their economic self-interest, resisted the reformers' efforts. A series of measures proposed by the British government in the 1820s to improve the conditions of the slaves, including restricting the use of the whip, limiting their work day to nine hours, and permitting them religious instruction, were rejected by the island's planter-dominated government. But Barbados was British territory, subject ultimately to London's dictate, and there, beyond the reach of the planters, the humanitarian movement for emancipation rolled on like a tidal wave in the British Parliament.

In 1833, Parliament acted. Effective the following year, on August 1, 1834, slavery would be abolished in British territory throughout the world. It was a momentous time: for the slaves, there was rejoicing, the end of "lick and lock up"; for the planters, dejection at the prospect of financial ruin; for Barbados as a whole, the end of a very long and lamentable era. But for Barbados, emancipation meant something else as well: it meant a beginning. From this day forward, with the recognition at long last of the *humanity* of three quarters of her people, Barbados' days as a mere island colony were at an end. Although she still had a long road to travel before all of her people, black and white, could be counted truly equal citizens, with emancipation Barbados had taken the first step of a journey which would lead to the creation of a nation.

Barbayduss

On the morning of August 1, 1834, Barbados awoke to the dawn of a new era.

For more than two hundred years—from the first day, in fact, of the establishment of the colony in 1627—Barbados had existed as a divided society, part slave, part free: a society in which those of African blood were denied recognition as full members of the human race. With emancipation, effective on that first day of August, the legal basis for that tragic denial disappeared. But for the island's black and coloured people, there remained ahead a long struggle for true acceptance as full members of Barbadian society. As that struggle evolved—and to a large extent as a result of that struggle—Barbados transformed itself from an island colony into a nation.

For all the concern and anguish that had preceded emancipation, when the freeing of the slaves actually came to pass it must have seemed an anticlimax, for it passed peaceably and without great fanfare. In part this was due to the fact that its coming had been known long in advance. The maturity of Barbados' slave population also played a role. But undoubtedly the most important element was the apprenticeship period of 4-6 years mandated by the Emancipation Act. As the name implies, this transitional period was intended to educate the slaves in the habits and traditions of citizenship, while at the same time ensuring the slave owners a reliable supply of labor until a wage system of labor evolved. During the apprenticeship, the former slaves were required to continue working for their former owner, with any work over the normal work week to be paid in wages. Many argued that Barbados' slaves had the competence for immediate freedom; at any rate the system was the source of continual strife between masters and apprentices, and in 1838 the apprenticeship system was ended for all slaves.

The end of the apprenticeship system brought dislocation to the uncomplicated labor supply the planters had known for generations: workers began moving from estate to estate, searching for the best wages and working conditions. And the response of the House of Assembly—the enactment of the Masters and Servants Act, creating the "located labor system"—was an indication that, although legal emancipation had arrived, Barbados was still very much under the domination of the planto-cracy which had held sway on the island since the end of the seventeenth century. The located labor system in effect bound a laborer to the plantation he had long worked for by permitting him to retain the house and garden plot he had occupied as a slave; the laborer in turn received a lower-than-market wage. This made it very difficult to seek a job elsewhere, because virtually all of the land on the island was bound up in the planta-tions, and there were no "free" villages with avail-able land or houses to which a worker might move. Furthermore, if a worker did move, he was liable to lose much or all of the produce in his garden plot, a vital consideration when nearly all the worker's sustenance and extra income came from such plots.

Of equal, if not greater, importance, however, were the rude facts of life for the laboring popula-tion: although the slaves had been given their legal freedom, they had been given nothing else—unlike the planters, who had received compensation from the British government for the loss of their chattel property when the slaves had been emancipated. Most of the former slaves had virtually nothing with which to start out in life as free men but their labor. And whether in bondage or as free men, there was little work for laborers in Barbados other than that on the sugar plantations. Indeed, even if there had been, the great mass of slaves had re-ceived little or no education of any kind, were illiterate, and untrained for anything other than the plantation work they had done all their lives.

So Barbados in the mid-nineteenth century was still a planter-dominated island; but, even in the nineteenth century, no island was completely an island. Barbados was subject to the same political and social winds affecting the outside world. And in that outside world, especially in England, the liberal and humanitarian view that rights lay with individuals, rather than with tradition and proper-ty, was gaining sway. In Barbados these views were championed by a growing middle class of whites and "free coloureds" (as they were known prior to emancipation) who had over time man-aged to satisfy the franchise requirements and who were beginning to make their presence felt on the political scene.

Their leader was a newspaper editor and politi-cian named Samuel Jackman Prescod, who rose from humble beginnings to become one of the outstanding figures in Barbadian history. The illegitimate son of a free coloured woman and a wealthy white planter, in 1843 Prescod became the first man of color to enter the hitherto all-white bastion of the House of Assembly. There and in his newspaper, the *Liberal*, he led the fight against racial and social discrimination, and against rule by and for the elite, seeking throughout his career to broaden the franchise so that the nominal freedom of the middle and lower classes might find political expression. Prescod and his followers met with only limited success: although over the ensuing decades partial steps to extend the vote would be taken, the struggle against the property qualification for voting would not be completely won until the middle of the twentieth century.

Remarkably, this protracted struggle was over-whelmingly peaceful, although in 1876 the tensions flowing from the continuing lopsidedness of politi-cal power (out of a population of 160,000 people, a mere 1300 men, mostly white and wealthy, had the right to vote) erupted in rioting. In the after-math, the property requirement for the franchise

As Barbados entered the 19th century, her devotion and attachment to things English continued undiminished: shortly after Admiral Nelson's victory and death at the battle of Trafalgar, a public subscription was begun for a statue to be placed in Bridgetown's main plaza, named Trafalgar Square in his honor.

Undiminished too was the role of sugar in the life of the island. Despite emancipation, which ended the slaves' legal bondage, economic reality kept the vast majority of former slaves tied to the life of the plantation and the cycle of planting, reaping, and grinding the crop. As throughout the West Indies, the planters of Barbados counted on the constant trade winds to power the windmills which ground the canes; at one point over 500 mills like the one above dotted the island.

During the mid- to late-19th century Barbados' most beloved architectural tradition came into being: the chattel house. Since virtually all the island's land was owned by the plantations, a worker's "house spot" was dependent on his employment; if he was fired or quit his job, he could be made to leave his house spot. Thus evolved the "chattel house"—a house which could be dismantled and moved from place to place. (The word "chattel" is the historic word for moveable property.)

With the social, economic, and legislative evolution of the later 20th century (a law passed in 1980 gave homeowners the right to buy their house spots very cheaply) the conditions which gave rise to the chattel house have faded. The classic chattel house of symmetrical form, gabled roof, and shuttered, wood-frame windows has become a rarer and rarer sight in the late 20th century, as homeowners "upgrade" their houses with such modernities as aluminum-framed louvered windows or verandas. Sadly for the nostalgic, the ultimate upgrade—a fixed house constructed of concrete block—is seen more and more across the countryside.

was reduced, at least on paper; but the reality was that this liberalization enabled very few additional voters to qualify because few owned sufficient property. Barbados' masses were discovering that although legislation had ended their bondage, altering the minds of men was an even more difficult process, especially when economic self-interest coincided with prejudice.

Nonetheless the nineteenth century did see progress in the social arena. The plantation owners had purposely denied education to their slaves: apart from its cost in both money and lost labor, the slave owners feared, no doubt rightly, that literacy would expose the slaves to liberal and abolitionist thinking. Perhaps for that very reason, when both religious and secular schools began opening from about 1830 on, the former slaves took to education with a passion. (A passion which, over time, did much to enlarge the middle class and which has remained with the Barbadian populace to this day.)

The arrival in 1825 of Barbados' first bishop, William Hart Coleridge, saw the Anglican Church begin serious efforts to reach out to and convert the black population, which it had long ignored. Although the Anglicans met with considerable success in these efforts, a de facto social discrimination within the church persisted well into the twentieth century. This no doubt contributed to the success of the many non-conformist denominations which began arriving in the island toward the end of the nineteenth century, and which actively proselytized among the masses. Their small churches, though lacking the stateliness of the stone Anglican parish churches, were soon to be found in virtually every village throughout the countryside, making religion easily accessible to the people.

This social evolution took place against a back-drop of severe economic distress, for the island's sugar industry was in decline from about 1865 on. Much of this depression was the result of external political and market forces, especially competition from subsidized European-grown beet sugar, but soil depletion and plant disease were also significant factors. The external market conditions would not improve until the turn of the century, but on the island itself two Barbadian researchers—J.R. Bovell and J. B. Harrison—made outstanding contributions which rescued the island's sugar industry. Most significant was the discovery, hitherto unknown to the world, of the ability of sugar cane to be grown from seed. This opened the way to breed hybrid varieties both resistant to disease and adapted to Barbados' growing conditions. (This pioneering work eventually led to the establishment of a sugar cane research station which today exports its hybrids and technology all over the world.)

Despite these and other advances in sugar technology, however, as Barbados entered the 20th century a central fact of Barbadian life remained unchanged: a very large majority of the island's working population were manual laborers employed in sugar, a crop subject to wild price swings and fierce international competition from countries where low wages were (and are) the rule. This reality, together with the concentration of ownership and wealth which was a continuing legacy of the plantation system, resulted in deplorable physical conditions for the overwhelming majority of the Bajan population. This was of course precisely the reality which had characterized Barbadian society throughout the eighteenth and nineteenth centuries, and very little had changed during those two hundred years. But a confluence of events and conditions in the twentieth century would bring enormous social, political,

Founded in 1628, Bridgetown soon became the economic and administrative center of the island, although Speightstown rivaled it as a port for shipping sugar in the early decades of the colony. Broad Street, seen here in a photograph circa 1900, runs westward from the Careenage. This strategic location near the city's gateway to the sea has long made it the city's principal shopping district.

During the slave era, plantation owners had discouraged or forbidden education and religion to their slaves, fearing that such exposure would encourage ideas of freedom; but with emancipation, schools and churches were gradually opened to the black population. The former slaves seized on education like a long-forbidden fruit, and this passion for education has remained strong in the Barbadian population to this day. (On the opposite page, a class of first-graders at the Clifton Hill Primary School in St. Thomas.)

The Anglican Church had been the island's dominant denomination since the founding of the colony, and even though freedom of religious expression had been guaranteed by the Charter of Barbados in 1652, other sects were often subject to severe discrimination. Religious tolerance grew during the nineteenth century: from the late 1800s a great many new denominations began establishing themselves on the island, and today virtually every village and neighborhood features at least one church [this page].

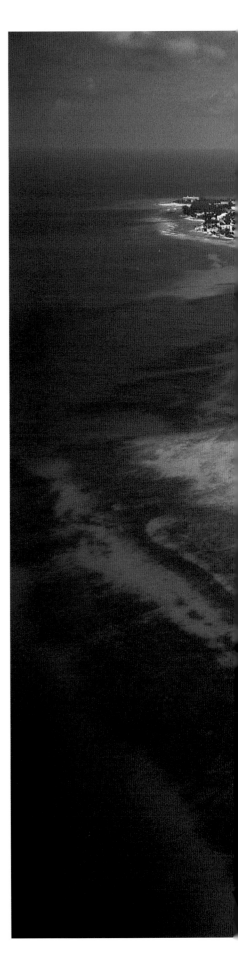

This century's changing social and economic conditions both in Barbados and throughout the world have brought the decline of the island's sugar industry, but as that historic industry has fallen, tourism has risen to take its place. The advent of the jetliner in the early 1960s transformed Barbados into a year-round tropical playground, and thousands of tourists flocked to the island to enjoy its superb beaches and surrounding waters. (The aerial view on the opposite page is of the Christ Church coast.)

With the steady decline in the fortunes of the sugar industry have come changes in Bajan life styles as well (partly as a result of that decline). One regrettable result has been the deterioration and abandonment of many of the island's historic plantation great houses, as their role as the centerpiece of plantation "worlds" has vanished.

Fortunately, new roles have been found for many of these magnificent houses, often in connection with Barbados' newly dominant industry, tourism. Among the fine examples of surviving great houses are the two pictured here: Francia [opposite page] was in the past open to visitors on a commercial basis, and was later converted into a private school. Bulkeley [above], one of Barbados' oldest plantation houses and a center of political power when "King Sugar" ruled the island, stands overlooking its lush lawn in the parish of St. George.

and economic change to the island.

Perhaps the most important factor in bringing about these changes was the increasing intrusion of the outside world and its ideas into the separate world that was Barbados. With advances in travel and communications, the planet has grown steadily smaller; and perhaps nowhere did this oft-cited observation apply with more force than on islands, where geography encourages and emphasizes insularity of thought. As has been mentioned in the discussion of emancipation, Barbados had never been totally isolated from the outside world, but with the 1900s came the first mass exposure of Barbadians to the world beyond its shores. And the first occasion for that exposure was, oddly enough, located in Panama.

The building of the Panama Canal by the United States would seem far removed from Barbadian social, economic, and political development, but in fact it affected all three. In need of a cheap, industrious work force adapted to the tropics, during the height of the project (1904-1914) the American government recruited tens of thousands of Barbadians to work in the isthmus. The "Panama Money" these workers sent back to the island was used for a variety of purposes, including the education of children. But probably the most consequential use was the purchase of thousands of small parcels of land and the building of homes on them by laboring-class Barbadians. Panama money thus bought the property qualification to vote imposed by the franchise laws, thereby greatly increasing the voting population, and in so doing laying the ground for legislative changes in the decades to come.

The Panama Canal experience, and then World War I, also opened the idea of working and living abroad to unprecedented numbers of Barbadians, and in the 1920s many of them would seek work in North America, where, in addition to higher wages, they would acquire new ideas about what they should expect in the political and economic realms. When some of these workers later returned to Barbados, they added their voices to the growing demand for change on the island.

The progressive social welfare ideas evolving in Europe and North America also were felt in the island legislature, and the 1920s saw the beginnings of legislation in the fields of health, pensions, and labor law. These trends were given a great push when in 1924 Charles Duncan O'Neal, who had studied and practiced medicine in the United Kingdom, returned home to Barbados and founded the Democratic League. The first political organization in Barbados' history aimed at organizing the masses, the League's goals included health and labor legislation, government support for education and housing, and the enlargement of the franchise.

It was in part because the restricted franchise limited avenues for political expression that the widespread destitution of the depression of the 1930s led to island-wide rioting in 1937, just as similar conditions had led to riots sixty years earlier. However, the aftermath of these riots would be very different from that of 1876, when very little real change had resulted.

In 1938 a group of Barbadians led by an Oxford-educated lawyer, Grantley (later Sir Grantley) Adams, formed the Barbados Labor Party (known for a time as the Barbados Progressive League), and called for a new era of government activism to improve the lot of the island's masses. The new organization's platform was virtually that of its forerunner, the Democratic League: reform and government assistance in education, health, housing, and in wages and working conditions. Three years later Adams and his colleagues formed the Barbados Workers' Union, which brought a new

The island's social and economic institutions evolved with increasing rapidity in this century, and so too did its political power. By mid-century the rapid transformation of the island from plantocracy to democracy was complete. As Barbados' people acquired political control over their own destiny, a sense of pride in their island identity took hold as well. In 1966 Bajans took the ultimate step toward that expression of identity by becoming an independent nation, and on November 30th of each year Barbados celebrates its nationhood with Independence Day festivities at the Garrison Savannah.

As Barbados has evolved from colony to independent country, two institutions have been in the forefront of inspiring the pride in heritage which has helped to forge a nation. The Barbados Museum [this page], located at the edge of the Garrison Savannah, contains an excellent collection depicting both the prehistorical and colonial eras. The museum is housed in the old Military Prison, which dates to the 1820s.

The Barbados National Trust has worked tirelessly to promote the preservation of the island's outstanding natural and architectural treasures. Members of the Trust's governing council pose before the Gun Hill Signal Station (erected in 1818), one of several historic landmark properties restored since the Trust's founding in 1961 [opposite page].

era to labor relations by giving the laboring class a collective voice and giving workers bargaining power commensurate with their employers.

At the head of his party in the House of Assembly, Adams spearheaded a veritable social revolution as much of the new party's program was enacted during the 1940s and '50s. A great deal of social legislation was still to come, but the foundation of the transformation Adams led was completed, and its survival guaranteed, when the long-sought prize, universal adult suffrage, was enacted in 1950. The dream Samuel Jackman Prescod had dreamed a century before—the enfranchisement of the emancipated—had at long last come to pass.

The Barbados Labour Party controlled the government until 1961 when the Democratic Labour Party, under the leadership of Errol Barrow, won election with a platform calling for government to play an even larger role in the economy. Five years later, Barrow's party sought and won reelection on a platform which included a call for independence from Great Britain; and so on November 30, 1966, after nearly three and a half centuries as a colony, Barbados became an independent country.

It had been a long road Barbados and Britain had traveled together since the founding of the colony. That road had not always been a smooth one, but each had always retained an overriding fondness and respect for the other. And so at independence, when Barbados decided to go her own way, it is not surprising that she decided as well to preserve that emotional link with her former guardian by remaining within the British Commonwealth.

That emotional link to the Mother Country has remained strong since independence, and "Bimshire" and "Little England" are still sometimes used as terms of endearment in referring to the island. It would be a mistake, however, to think that Barbados remains somehow an English appendage. The three and a half centuries of Barbados' existence have molded a distinct people, with a unique culture created from a blend of England and Africa. *"Los Barbados"* the island had been to the Spanish and Portuguese; "Little England" and "Bimshire" she became during her centuries as a colony; but to her people today, in the unique language of the island, she is simply "Barbayduss." Out of time and struggle a nation and a people were born, and they proudly—and luckily—remain a special world, a world apart.

Sun, Sea & Sugar

O, island in the sun . . .. The sun, sea, and sand of a tropical playground make up the image Barbados presents to the world today. But if and when visitors to the island steal some time from the beach to do a bit of exploring, a fourth "s" becomes apparent as they drive around the countryside: sugar cane. Although understandable, it is also ironic that sugar comes to the visitor's mind only as an afterthought, because for three centuries Barbados *was* sugar.

From the middle of the seventeenth century, when it was first introduced to the island, until well into the twentieth, sugar ordained the island's economy, people, society, and government. Even to this day—although one must wonder for how much longer—cane fields dominate the island's appearance, a sea of green ruffling gently in the trade winds. For those who have known Barbados for many years, it is hard to conceive of the island without its yellow-green carpet contrasting with the blue of sea and sky. But in the final years of the twentieth century the notion of Barbados without sugar cane has become a very real possibility.

Not that Barbadians have not tried, over the years, to diversify into other crops: tobacco, ginger, cotton, and, more recently, papayas, flowers and vegetables have all been tried, not without some success. But the fact is that the crop which Barbados in a sense stumbled onto in 1637 is extraordinarily suited to the island's topography, soil, and climate; and sugar cane, in turn, is perhaps irreplaceable from a commercial and environmental standpoint, because it is unmatched at anchoring the island's thin soil against the trade winds and sometimes-torrential rains.

Indeed, the most successful "crop" which Barbados has found to supplant sugar cane's role is the one grown on her beaches: tourism. Fortunately for the island, tourism began to boom just as the sugar industry began a precipitous decline. Barbados had received a certain number of winter visitors since the early 1900s, but it is only since the 1960s, with the cheap and rapid air travel made possible by the jetliner, that the island's climate, natural features and setting have become accessible to large numbers of people. The development of the jet coincided with two further post-war essentials: the growth of a large, affluent middle class in North America (and, to a lesser extent, in Europe), and a newfound fondness for going out in the blazing sun to get a tan. The result has been not only the establishment of tourism as the major industry for the Barbadian economy, but the exposure of Barbadian society to the outside world to a degree that this tiny island had never before experienced.

On a St. Andrew hillside overlooking the Scotland District, the Morgan Lewis Windmill [this page] is the only windmill surviving in Barbados complete with arms and cane grinding machinery (the restored mill lacks only the canvas sails which caught the wind). Once upon a time over 500 such windmills dotted the island, and many continued functioning well into the 20th century, when steam-powered factories completed the takeover of grinding the cane.

Although "King Sugar" ruled for more than three centuries and cane fields continue to dominate the landscape, the island's sugar industry has been in steep decline since the 1950s. Whether this scene [opposite page], so long a part of Barbados' history, will long endure is very much open to question.

As the island's sugar industry has shrunk, much of the land near Bridgetown, which was historically planted in sugar cane, has been developed for industrial, commercial, and residential use. Fortunately, the dramatic east coast [seen above] has been spared this development, and looks today much as it has for eons.

The decline of the sugar industry has been matched by the rise of tourism: in 1968 tourist revenues overtook sugar exports as the country's number one foreign exchange earner. (On the opposite page is St. Philip's Crane Beach, widely regarded as one of the finest beaches in the world.)

Lured by mild tropical weather and warm ocean temperature the year around, tourist arrivals grew steadily in the '60s and '70s. Fluctuating arrival levels since those heady growth years have led to efforts to broaden the island's tourist appeal, and developers have plans for luring more golfers with new courses to add to the excellent eighteen holes at Sandy Lane, near Holetown [this page].

Two shiploads of merry-makers head for port after an afternoon on the Jolly Roger "fun cruises" off the west coast [opposite page].

Although Barbados has historically drawn most of its tourists from North America, recent years have seen a boom in visitors from new markets such as Europe and Latin America. (Above and opposite, the beauties of the beaches on St. Peter's west coast.)

Rain-laden easterly trade winds sweeping onto Barbados from the Atlantic Ocean have created the most dramatic scenery on the island's sparsely-populated east coast, seen here [this page] looking north from a point near Bathsheba.

Near Foster Hall [opposite page], to the south of Bathsheba, a double row of palms frames a country highway descending toward the east coast.

Although the island's tourism is predominantly focused on its sun, sand, and sea, a number of the island's historic "great houses" are open to visitors on a regular basis, giving visitors a chance to explore the architecture and lifestyle of the "King Sugar" era. Among the most striking of these houses is St. Nicholas Abbey in St. Peter (shown in "England & Africa") and Sunbury Plantation House in St. Philip [these pages].

Like many of Barbados' great houses, Sunbury is of uncertain date. It is known to have survived the great hurricane of 1780, and may date from as early as the second half of the 17th century. In addition to its superb drawing room [above], Sunbury boasts the island's largest collection of horse-drawn vehicles, as well as an enormous assemblage of plantation-era artifacts.

The old and the new in tourism: near the southeastern corner of the island, historic Sam Lord's Castle [above] was built in 1820 by Samuel Hall Lord. According to legend (although, alas, for the lovers of legend, no hard evidence), Sam Lord acquired his fortune as a "wrecker," by luring unsuspecting ship captains onto reefs with false harbor lights placed in coconut trees. This shot was taken in 1993, when the mansion was in the midst of its glory days, serving as the centerpiece for a large resort hotel.

A luxury cruise ship docked in Bridgetown's Deep Water Harbour represents the growing trend in Caribbean tourism [opposite page].

A catamaran decorates a Christ Church beach.

Bridgetown

Surrounded by water, Barbados nonetheless has only one real gateway to the sea, at the mouth of the tiny stream named, with considerable imaginative license, the Constitution River. Thus it was here in 1628, at what came to be called the Careenage, that the colonizers established a town, naming it for the remains of the rustic Indian bridge which they found across the stream. (Indeed, in the early years of the colony, the settlement was sometimes called "The Indian Bridge Towne"; among its other names before "Bridgetown" was finally settled on were "St. Michael's Town," "The Bridge," and "The Bridge-town.")

Although it has a small-town feel, the city is home to over 100,000 people, when the contiguous surrounding urban area is included—about forty percent of the island's population. Undoubtedly much of that small-town feel is due to the fact that so many people know each other, and greetings are constantly heard in the street, for the city remains as much the country's social crossroads as it is the center of commerce. In fact the growth of the middle class and the spread of automobile ownership in the last two decades have brought with them (in addition to traffic jams and car parks) a diminished importance for the city center as the hub of com-merce, as supermarkets, shops, branch offices, and shopping centers have sprung up in the suburbs and outlying areas.

Although the city as an entity is approaching four centuries of existence and is therefore ancient by New World standards, due to the use of wood in early construction, coupled with repeated, devastating fires and less frequent but equally devastating hurricanes (in 1675, 1780, and 1831), very few of its buildings are. With only a handful of exceptions, the buildings of Bridgetown do not pre-date the mid-nineteenth century.

Nonetheless, the city has an aged air to it, thanks in part to the many wooden and iron balconies over-hanging the streets; thanks also, regrettably, to the preventable deterioration of many older buildings, which is often a prelude to their demolition. Those who have known Broad Street far longer than I speak nostalgically of the many classic façades which were torn down in recent decades in a blind rush to the "modern." Thus it is heartening to see the growing awareness of the beauty of Barbados' traditional architectural styles, and the recent efforts to restore some splendid buildings to their original lustre (for a detail of one example, see the final photograph of this chapter).

Bridgetown spreads out from the Careenage, the harbor which gave it birth in 1628.

At the heart of the city lie the Careenage, National Heroes Square, and the Parliament Buildings (right side of the photograph). The Careenage takes its name from times past when wooden boats were hauled to the edge of the narrow waterway and "careened," or leaned on their sides, to clean and repair their hulls. At the far edge of the small grassy park is the Cenotaph, honoring the island's war dead; on the far side of Heroes Square (for decades known as Trafalgar Square) stands the statue of Admiral Nelson, with Broad Street stretching beyond. At the right of the photograph are the two Parliament Buildings, which have housed the island's legislature since the 1870s.

Parishioners come and go for Sunday services at St. Michael's Cathedral [this page], which dates from 1786. Anglicanism has historically been the dominant religion of the island; today the island counts dozens of denominations and faiths.

Jews were among the earliest of the colony's settlers, having arrived in the year after the colony's founding; in the following decades they figured prominently in the development of the island's sugar industry. Around 1654, when they were first given permission to worship publicly, the island's Jews built a synagogue in Bridgetown which survived until the great hurricane of 1831. Two years later a new synagogue was completed, but this fell into disrepair during the 1930s, following the emigration of most of the island's Jews. After a superb rescue effort begun in 1983 by a revitalized Jewish community, the beautifully-restored Synagogue stands on Synagogue Lane [opposite page] much as it looked a century and a half ago.

Bridgetown boasts a great range of architectural styles, both old and modern, but due to devastating fires and hurricanes during the seventeenth, eighteenth, and nineteenth centuries, very few of its buildings pre-date the 1850s. One of the most striking of the older survivors is the Barbados Mutual Life Assurance Company Building on Lower Broad Street [this page], which dates from 1895.

One of the city's newest structures, the Central Bank Building's ten stories make it the tallest building on the island; it houses a large concert hall in addition to its banking offices [opposite page].

Bridgetown, like the country as a whole, has undergone enormous changes in the three decades I have known it; as a photographer, I seldom see "progress" as an unalloyed good, for it often comes at the expense of destroying much of what makes a place architecturally and culturally picturesque and charming. The photographs on these pages are a few of the scenes I captured during the 1980s, including the sidewalk fruit and vegetable vendors (virtually all of them women) who enlivened much of central Bridgetown for decades. (My files contain few such photographs, for, with rare exceptions, my requests to photograph these vendors nearly always met with refusal.)

One of the city's main thoroughfares, Baxter's Road [opposite page] preserves the architectural style of an earlier era. The street is famous for the sidewalk food vendors who keep the street alive into the wee hours of the morning.

As the city has outgrown its traditional boundaries, once-residential areas have lately become new centers of commerce; in the process many buildings originally built as homes have been transformed into commercial establishments, like this fine example on Highway 7 in Christ Church [this page].

Broad Street remains Bridgetown's principal commercial district, as it has been since the earliest days of the city, when the street's name doubtless seemed more fitting. The street is lined with the main offices and stores of many of the country's banks and retailers, and although many of the historic buildings of yesteryear have been demolished or modernized out of existence, a few architectural gems such as this one remain.

Bajan

One of the most complex and difficult aspects of putting a book like this together is deciding what is to be included and what must be left out. I refer here not only to the actual editing process, but to the original coverage itself: that is, what to photograph and research. To a great extent, this is for me an intuitive process, arrived at almost through an unconscious, osmotic process over the period of months I typically spend in a place doing the photography and research for one of my books.

It is relatively easy, although time-consuming, to photograph the physical aspects of a place; very much harder to capture its essence: its culture, people, values—in short, the very things that make a particular place unique, or, in the words of the subtitle, *A World Apart*. Despite the difficulty of recording on film those more subtle aspects of a given locale, I have never been content to produce a book which shows only beautiful landscapes, beaches, and palm trees; indeed, I would consider any such book of mine to be a failure, for it has always been my intention, and certainly my hope, that my books should educate as well as entertain.

A further complexity involves the organization of the photographs that are finally chosen: some fall logically into categories, and these become sections or chapters. Others are not so easily classified, and yet they communicate something which I find captivating and essential to the personality of a place. Many of those photographs are scattered throughout this book, especially in the historical sections. But I invariably find, when it comes to finally laying out the book, that I have photographs that fit into no neat category but which are nonetheless vital to conveying part of the essence of the world I am attempting to capture and describe.

Hence this section, and the opportunity for a note about the meaning of "Bajan": to the casual visitor, it may merely evoke beautiful beaches, chattel houses, and fields of sugar cane. To me, however, it means above all a style of living, shaped by a small island in the Caribbean; and it brings to my mind the limitations inherent in the phrases "per capita income" and "standard of living" as they are normally employed. Such statistics classify Barbados as a "developing country," and imply that it must "catch up" to the standards of North America and Western Europe. What the statistics cannot convey is an approach to life which embraces a beautiful land and climate, values community above material possessions, and each day for itself, rather than as merely a means to an end. It is a way of looking at life from which the "developed" world could learn a great deal.

A final note for the uninitiated: "Bajan" (pronounced BAY-jun), is the diminutive for Barbadian, and is used interchangeably with the longer word.

Mild tropical weather the year around support a profusion of flowers, and two public gardens—Andromeda and the Flower Forest, both in the parish of St. Joseph (where the allamanda, seen on this page, and an oleander, opposite, were photographed)— provide beautiful displays of the gardener's craft.

Often mistaken for goats by visitors, blackbelly sheep are a common sight staked out along roadsides, and are so well adapted to tropical climates that the island does a substantial business in exporting breeding stock. The breed evolved in Barbados genera-tions ago from a cross between a European wool sheep and an African "hair" sheep.

Far less often seen, the Barbados green monkey has an island pedigree as old as the blackbelly's, for it was introduced to the island during the slave era, when sailors' pets picked up in Africa took to the wild in Barbados. Long considered an agricultural pest, the monkeys have recently become valued as both research animals and for tourism, being the star attraction at the Barbados Wildlife Reserve in St. Peter.

A cricket match enlivens a Saturday afternoon in Christ Church [this page]. It is sometimes claimed that cricket is the true religion of Barbados and the West Indies, and there is no doubting the unifying and leveling role it has played in Bajan society over the past century. There is also no doubt that at the spectator level the game remains the passion of Barbadian sports-lovers, although some would argue that in number of participants it is being surpassed by today's true world sport, basketball.

Perhaps dreaming of future days of greatness, a young player awaits his turn at bat during a Saturday afternoon cricket match in Queen's Park [opposite page].

If cricket has historically been Barbados' unifying force, then it can equally be said that it is through calypso that today's most forceful voices of social and political commentary are heard. Undoubtedly the most famous of these voices is that of Mighty Gabby [this page]. While many of his songs consist of hard-hitting political criticism, perhaps his most touching music is a celebration of traditional Bajan culture.

A master of social observation in a more traditional medium, writer George Lamming [opposite page] has explored many of the complexities of modern West Indian life in his many novels, essays, and poetry. At the core of his writing—much of it autobiographical—are the moral challenges posed by the cultural tensions arising from colonialism and its aftermath. As is the case with many Caribbean writers, Lamming's analysis of life in the West Indies has been shaped and sharpened by living abroad, both in England and the United States.

Kadooment Day revelers parade through the streets of Bridgetown, bringing another Crop Over festival to a close [this page]. An annual summer celebration of culture and merriment, the modern Crop Over reincarnates the celebrations traditionally held on the island's sugar plantations when the last of the crop had been brought in. Through the calypso competition which is a central element of the festival, Crop Over has made an important contribution to the rebirth of the island's now-dominant musical form.

Another of the island's occasions for merriment is the Oistins Fish Festival, held annually during Easter week, where a tuk band complete with "donkey man" entertains the crowd [opposite page]. Unique to Barbados, the music of the tuk band's drums and tin flute also owes its origins to the plantation era, when slaves traditionally held Sunday dances.

Two essential elements of Bajan life: horse racing at the Garrison Savannah and the neighborhood domino game. Racing at the Garrison [opposite page] dates from the mid-1800s. Like many things Barbadian, Bajan horse racing offers a special twist: races I witnessed during my stays on the island included the spectacle of enthusiastic fans surging onto the track to urge their favorites on as they headed down the home stretch!

Every rum shop, sidewalk, and quiet corner is likely to host a domino game at some time during the day or night [this page].

Postcards

&

Postscripts

Although I by no means consider myself an "old Barbados hand," the fifteen years that I have been coming to the island has been long enough to see substantial changes take place. When I first came to the island, for example, the ABC Highway had not yet been built, and the number of cars on the road was but a fraction of what it is today. Imagine, then, my amused amazement on my final visit to take photographs for this book when I first heard the radio reports of "Skyrider," the airborne reporter announcing the morning rush-hour traffic conditions from his Cessna—something I take for granted in my native California but hardly expected in little Barbados.

The fact is, of course, that my "little Barbados," the Barbados I got to know in the late 1970s, is constantly changing; and as with a child one sees only occasionally, the changes can be startling. Every time I visit the island there are new buildings, widened highways, new developments. Of course this means that some of the old architectural "characters" I remembered with fondness have vanished, although I am happy to say that the past fifteen years have brought a tremendously

heightened awareness of the value of Barbados' architectural and cultural tradition. Much of this has been fostered, and all of it encouraged, by organizations like the Barbados National Trust and the Barbados Museum & Historical Society (both featured in an earlier chapter). The island's government, too, responding to increased concern on the part of the general public, has assumed a more active role in preserving the country's cultural and architectural patrimony.

Despite these efforts, I know the island will continue to change, and rightly so: for Barbados is a vibrant, dynamic society, not a sort of Caribbean island Disneyland where all is preserved as it was the last time you visited. The world changes, and Barbados must change with it, dealing with the problems confronting it as it attempts to create a better life for all its people.

Because Barbados has changed, and will continue to change, I have included in this closing section of some of my favorite photographs, a few pictures of a bygone Barbados, the Barbados I have known over the past decade and a half, and which lives on fondly in my memory.

Within the memory of many living Barbadians the donkey cart was still a common sight. They have now almost completely disappeared, but a very few hang on, like this one I photographed on Bay Street in the mid-1980s, carrying miscellaneous freight and their aged owners, and adding color to the Bajan landscape.

Rosa and Swan *wait patiently on a lonely St. James Beach on the west coast [above].   The Careenage [opposite page] has been at the heart of Bridgetown since 1628, when the colonists founded a settlement near its banks. Its role has changed over the years: before the construction of the Deep Water Harbour in 1961, it teemed with lighters ferrying sugar and other cargo to large ships anchored in Carlisle Bay. As late as the 1970s and '80s it was home to Bridgetown's large fleet of day fishing boats, most of which now call at other ports on the island.*

Although there appears to be no precise count of the number of "rum shops" on the island (and anyway it would be wrong by the time this is read), one source states that there are about 1600, and that seems close enough. Whatever the number, they are an essential ingredient of every neighborhood, village, and hamlet, and dispense small grocery items and communal good cheer in addition to rum. Ernetta Edghill, the proprietress, runs "The Wee Wee Shop" in Foul Bay, St. Philip [this page].

Although the benefits of progress for the island are undeniable, there have been casualties as well, including some of the most colorful architecture of Bridgetown. The "John Bull Bar," just off Broad Street [opposite page], made way for a modern building sometime in the nineteen eighties.

Barbados is blessed with a good number of concerned people who labor strenuously to preserve the island's cultural and architectural heritage, but no one has done more to popularize the inherent beauty and charm of Barbados' ordinary houses, shops, and commercial buildings than artist Jill Walker (posed above at the gate to her home and studio at Welches, a restored eighteenth-century plantation house). Although her paintings of chattel houses and other Barbadian scenes [opposite page] have proved enormously popular with visitors, they have struck a chord with Bajans as well, and her art is regularly seen in homes and offices throughout the island.

In 1975 she and her husband, architect Jimmy Walker, opened Best of Barbados, a shop featuring her prints and designs; in the ensuing years her art has proved so popular that that single original store has grown into the largest chain of gift shops on the island.

The prints on this page are by, copyright of, and courtesy of Jill Walker. Used by permission.

A group of St. Lucy schoolchildren giggle for the photographer while waiting for their morning ride to school [this page].

An image from the past, Harbour Police Constable Vernon Garnes wears a uniform whose design dates to the English Navy of the eighteenth century [opposite page].

The fishing fleet in Oistins Bay [this page] rides a gentle evening swell as a tropical sunset lights the sky over the south coast. Symbols of the island, a row of cabbage palms salute the sun slipping toward the sea on the western horizon [opposite page].

Notes

1. Acknowledgements: Barbadians are an exceedingly open and gracious people, and this book owes much to that national personality; more times than I can remember, people have given me (often as a total stranger) access to their homes, property, records, and time to facilitate my photography or research. Beyond these casual and often fleeting encounters, I am deeply indebted to the following—a number of whom I am privileged to call my friends—for the information, background, guidance, assistance, and hospitality they generously extended over the months I spent preparing this book: Kathleen Goddard, for unstinting encouragement, advice, and help in making contact with people through her legion of friends; Jimmy and Jill Walker, Chris and Susan Trew, and all the people at Best of Barbados; Jeremy and Jenny Sisnet; Henry Fraser, Paul Foster, and Paul Altman, all of the Barbados National Trust; Barbados Museum & Historical Society; Barbados Board of Tourism; Jean and Suzanne Baulu; Pastor John Jones and congregation of the New Testament Church of God, Sweet Vale, St. George; Canon E.L. Payne, St. John's Parish Church; Walter Murray Chiesa; Jimmy Walker, Warren Alleyne, Ella LaBrucherie, and Howard Rhodes for reviewing and commenting on the text; Modern Graphics; Martha Hoch, for assisting with the picture selection, artwork, design, and layout; and finally, the late Thomas H. King, Jr., a friend since our Peace Corps days together, whose extraordinary hospitality many years ago made my first two books on the island possible, and laid the foundation for this one.

2. Sources: My acquaintance with Barbados began in 1978, when I spent several months photographing the island for my first book, *Images of Barbados*. I say acquaintance advisedly (and, I trust people will believe, without false modesty) because I know how limited my knowledge of Barbados is. Although I have, over the past fifteen years, spent many months and uncounted hours driving minimokes, cars, and motorcycles all over the island in search of photographs and an understanding of Barbados, I know full well that the bulk of my knowledge of the island is visual and the knowledge of an outsider.

I consider myself very fortunate, therefore, to have been able to refer to and rely on a number of excellent books to fill gaps in my knowledge. I recommend all of the following works to the reader seeking a fuller understanding of Barbados: Fraser, Carrington, Forde, & Gilmore, *A-Z of Barbadian Heritage*; Hilary Beckles, *A History of Barbados*; Rachel Wilder, *Insight Guides: Barbados*; F.A. Hoyos, *Barbados, A History . . .*; Warren Alleyne, *Historic Bridgetown*; and Ronald Tree, *A History of Barbados*. Additionally, the thoughts and writings of commentators such as Phillip Goddard, Gladstone Holder, Ronald Hughes, and Woodville Marshall have added significantly to my understanding of the island.

3. Photographic notes: The photographs for this book were shot on Kodachrome film, both 25 and 64 ASA. I have, over the years, worked with a number of color films, but for overall quality of both the filmstock and processing, I have yet to find films to surpass the Kodachromes. (When photographing for reproduction, transparency films are usually preferred over print films.) My equipment consisted of 35mm Nikon cameras (two FE's and an F3, all with motor drives) and eleven Nikkor lenses ranging from 16mm to 300mm in focal length. Most exposures were made based on the in-camera light meters, although I sometimes use a spot meter and an incident meter in difficult lighting conditions.

4. Picture Credits: All photographs and illustrations are by the author except: p. 3: The Library of Congress, Washington, D.C.; p. 34: The Granger Collection, New York; p. 37: The Mansell Collection, London; p. 40: The Houghton Library, Harvard College; pp. 44, 48-49, 51: The Barbados Museum & Historical Society; p. 57: courtesy of The Beinecke Collection, Hamilton College Library; p. 61: The Barbados Museum & Historical Society; p. 64: James Forde; p. 80: Vince Cavataio; p. 83: courtesy of 1627 & All That; p. 123: courtesy and copyright of Jill Walker.

Company Sponsors

The publishers gratefully acknowledge the generous financial support of the following companies, which has assisted this book to publication:

Banks (Barbados) Breweries, Ltd.
Barbados External Telecommunications Ltd.
Best of Barbados Limited
British-American Tobacco (Barbados) Ltd.
Chickmont Foods Ltd.
Coopers and Lybrand
C. O. Williams Construction Ltd.
C. O. Williams Electrical Ltd.
Kodak Caribbean Limited
Melville and Company Limited

© 2006 Roger A. LaBrucherie

Imágenes Press
Post Office Box 1150
Pine Valley, California 91962 USA
Tel: (619) 473-8676 or (619) 997-8676
Email: imagenespress@aol.com

Design consultant: Geneva Design Studio

Barbados, A World Apart
(Revised Edition)
ISBN 0-939302-40-3

Printed in China

Discovery and settlement: Barbados was inhabited by Indians from South America for centuries prior to the arrival of Europeans in the New World. The island was uninhabited in 1625, however, when it was claimed for England; two years later the English established their first settlement, and the island remained a British colony without interruption until Barbados became an independent nation on November 30, 1966. The name of the island means "bearded" in both Spanish and Portuguese, and is thought to derive from the bearded fig trees indigenous to the island. The name is pronounced "Bar-BAY-dohs" outside the island, although in the distinctive speech of the island it is usually pronounced "Bar-BAY-duss" by Barbadians themselves.

Geography and topography: Easternmost of the Caribbean islands, Barbados lies approximately 100 miles (160 km) to the east of the Windward Chain and about 200 miles (320 km) northeast of Trinidad at 13m 15' N., 59m 30' W. The island measures 21 miles (34 km) long by 14 miles (22 km) wide at its widest point, with a surface area of 166 sq. miles (431 sq. km). Its coral surface is generally hilly in aspect, rising in a series of terraces to the island's highest point, 1116 feet (340 m) above sea level, at Mt. Hillaby.

Population: 280,000 (2006 est.), about half of which is concentrated in the metropolitan Bridgetown area. Population density is one of the highest in the world for a country (approx. 1700 per sq. mile). Ethnically, the population is approximately 80% African, 16% mixed, 4% Caucasian. Life expectancy is 75 years. Education is free and compulsory to the age of 16; adult literacy is about 97%.

Government: Formerly a British Colony, Barbados has been an independent, democratic nation within the British Commonwealth since 1966. Barbados' government is headed by a Prime Minister under a British-patterned parliamentary system, elected under universal adult suffrage. The Governor General represents the British monarch, who is head of state.

Economy: Barbados was historically a sugar monoculture, but sugar production has been surpassed in importance by tourism and manufacturing, with strong growth in offshore finance and information services in recent years. Gross domestic product per capita is about US$17,400 (2005 est.).

Climate: Mild-tropical, moderated by near-constant easterly trade winds; temperatures ranges from 75-84°F. (24-29°C.); annual rainfall is about 60" (152 cm), heaviest during June-November.

Miscellaneous: Language: English. Religion: historically the Anglican church predominated, but complete freedom of religion prevails today, and more than two dozen faiths are now represented. Motto: Pride and Industry. National flower: Pride of Barbados (Caesalpinia pulcherrima).

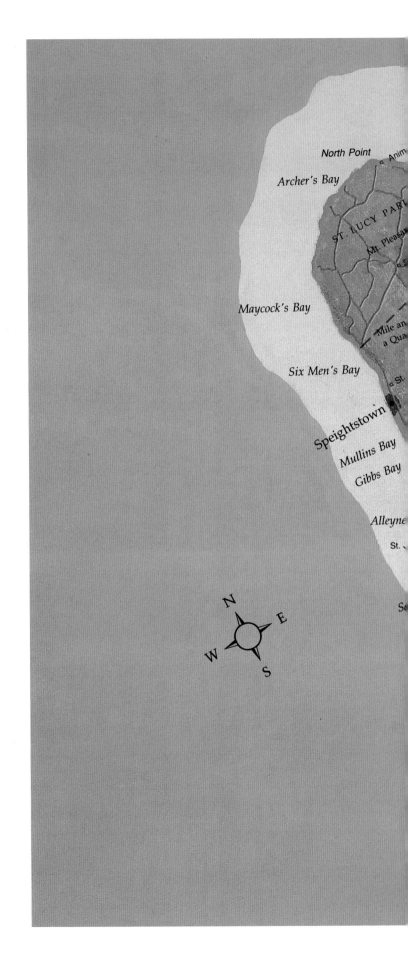

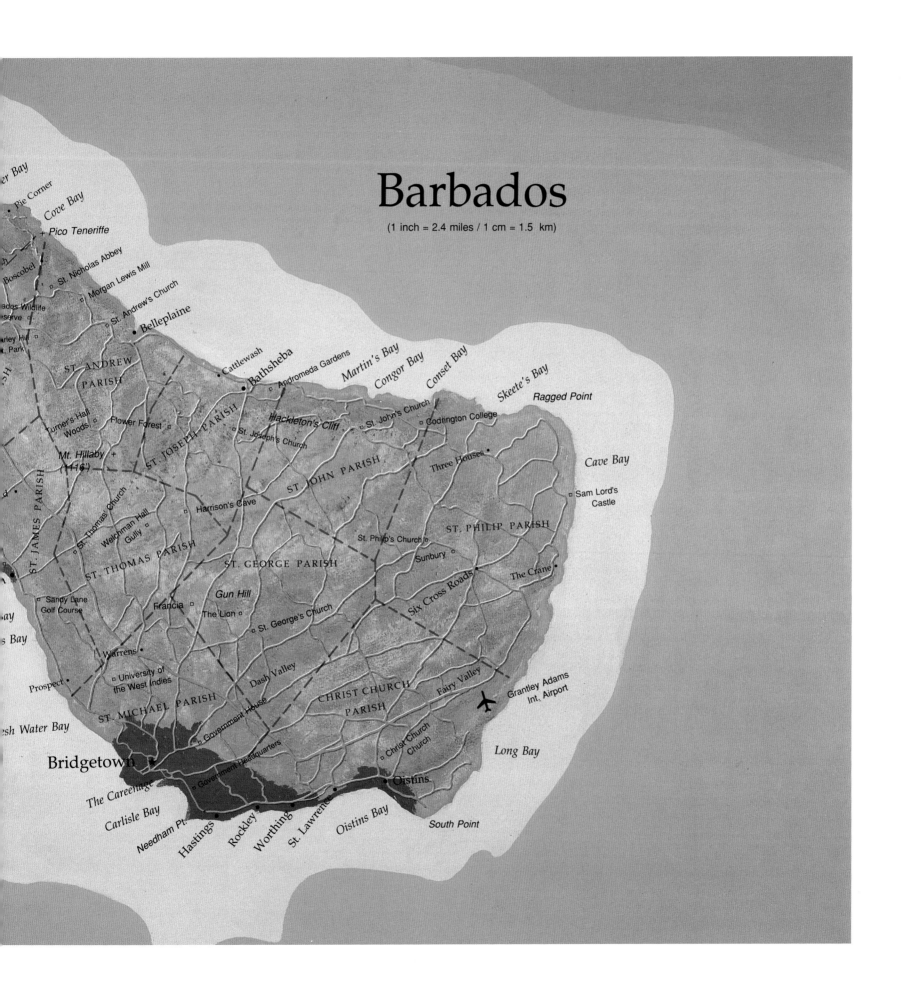

Barbados

(1 inch = 2.4 miles / 1 cm = 1.5 km)

Pie Corner

Cove Bay

+ Pico Teneriffe

Boscobel

St. Nicholas Abbey

Morgan Lewis Mill

ados Wildlife
serve

St. Andrew's Church

Belleplaine

arley Hill
, Park

ST. ANDREW
PARISH

Cattlewash

Bathsheba

Andromeda Gardens

Martin's Bay

Congor Bay

Conset Bay

Skeete's Bay

Ragged Point

Turner's Hall
Woods

Flower Forest

Hackleton's Cliff

St. John's Church

Codrington College

St. Joseph's Church

Cave Bay

Mt. Hillaby +
(1116')

ST. JOSEPH PARISH

ST. JOHN PARISH

Three Houses

Sam Lord's
Castle

ST. JAMES PARISH

Harrison's Cave

St. Thomas Church

Welchman Hall
Gully

St. Philip's Church

ST. PHILIP PARISH

ST. THOMAS PARISH

ST. GEORGE PARISH

Sunbury

The Crane

Sandy Lane
Golf Course

Francia

Gun Hill

Six Cross Roads

ay

The Lion

St. George's Church

s Bay

Warrens

University of
the West Indies

Dash Valley

Fairy Valley

Grantley Adams
Int. Airport

Prospect

ST. MICHAEL PARISH

Government House

CHRIST CHURCH
PARISH

sh Water Bay

Bridgetown

Government Headquarters

Christ Church
Church

Long Bay

The Careenage

Oistins

Carlisle Bay

Needham Pt.

Hastings

Rockley

Worthing

St. Lawrence

Oistins Bay

South Point

Sunset on the west coast at Alleynes Bay, St. James